Drama for Students, Volume 3

Staff

Editorial: David M. Galens, *Editor*. Terry Browne, Christopher Busiel, Clare Cross, Tom Faulkner, John Fiero, David M. Galens, Carole Hamilton, Sheri Metzger, Daniel Moran, Terry Nienhuis, William P. Wiles, Joanne Woolway, Etta Worthington, *Entry Writers*. Elizabeth Cranston, Kathleen J. Edgar, Jennifer Gariepy, Dwayne D. Hayes, Kurt Kuban, Joshua Kondek, Tom Ligotti, Scot Peacock, Patti Tippett, Pam Zuber, *Contributing Editors*. James Draper, *Managing Editor*. Diane Telgen, *"For Students" Line Coordinator*. Jeffery Chapman, *Programmer/Analyst*.

Research: Victoria B. Cariappa, *Research Team Manager*. Andy Malonis, Barb McNeil, *Research Specialists*. Julia C. Daniel, Tamara C. Nott, Tracie A. Richardson, Cheryl L. Warnock, *Research Associates*. Phyllis P. Blackman, Jeffrey D. Daniels,

Corrine A. Stocker, *Research Assistants*.

Permissions: Susan M. Trosky, *Permissions Manager*. Kimberly F. Smilay, *Permissions Specialist*. Steve Cusack and Kelly A. Quin, *Permissions Associates*.

Production: Mary Beth Trimper, *Production Director*. Evi Seoud, *Assistant Production Manager*. Shanna Heilveil, *Production Assistant*.

Graphic Services: Randy Bassett, *Image Database Supervisor*. Robert Duncan and Michael Logusz, *Imaging Specialists*. Pamela A. Reed, *Photography Coordinator*. Gary Leach, *Macintosh Artist*.

Product Design: Cynthia Baldwin, *Product Design Manager*. Cover Design: Michelle DiMercurio, *Art Director*. Page Design: Pamela A. E. Galbreath, *Senior Art Director*.

Copyright Notice

Since this page cannot legibly accommodate all copyright notices, the acknowledgments constitute an extension of the copyright notice.

While every effort has been made to secure permission to reprint material and to ensure the reliability of the information presented in this publication, Gale Research neither guarantees the accuracy of the data contained herein nor assumes any responsibility for errors, omissions, or discrepancies. Gale accepts no payment for listing; and inclusion in the publication of any organization, agency, institution, publication, service, or individual does not imply endorsement of the editors or publisher. Errors brought to the attention of the publisher and verified to the satisfaction of the publisher will be corrected in future editions.

This publication is a creative work fully protected by all applicable copyright laws, as well as by misappropriation, trade secret, unfair competition, and other applicable laws. The authors and editors of this work have added value to the underlying factual material herein through one or more of the following: unique and original selection, coordination, expression, arrangement, and classification of information. All rights to this publication will be vigorously defended.

Copyright © 1998
Gale Research
835 Penobscot Building
645 Griswold
Detroit, MI 48226-4094

This book is printed on acid-free paper that meets the minimum requirements of American National Standard for Information Sciences—Permanence Paper for Printed Library Materials, ANSI Z39.48-1984.

ISBN 0-7876-2752-6
ISSN 1094-9232

Printed in the United States of America
10 9 8 7 6 5 4 3 2

The Crucible

Arthur Miller

1953

Introduction

Using the historical subject of the Salem Witch trials, Arthur Miller's play *The Crucible* (1953) presents an allegory for events in contemporary America. The Salem Witch Trials took place in Salem, Massachusetts in 1692, and were based on the accusations of a twelve-year-old girl named Anne Putnam. Putnam claimed that she had witnessed a number of Salem's residents holding black sabbaths and consorting with Satan. Based on these accusations, an English-American clergyman named Samuel Parris spearheaded the prosecution of dozens of alleged witches in the Massachusetts colony. Nineteen people were hanged and one pressed to death over the following two years.

Miller's play employs these historical events to criticize the moments in humankind's history when reason and fact became clouded by irrational fears and the desire to place the blame for society's problems on others. Dealing with elements such as false accusations, manifestations of mass hysteria, and rumor-mongering, *The Crucible* is seen by many as more of a commentary on "McCarthyism" than the actual Salem trials. "McCarthyism" was the name given to a movement led by Senator Joe McCarthy and his House Committee on Un-American Activities. This movement involved the hunting down and exposing of people suspected of having communist sympathies or connections. While those found guilty in McCarthy's witch hunt were not executed, many suffered irreparable damage to their reputations. Miller himself came under suspicion during this time.

While *The Crucible* achieved its greatest resonance in the 1950s—when McCarthy's reign of terror was still fresh in the public's mind—Miller's work has elements that have continued to provoke and enthrall audiences. That the play works on a wider allegorical level is suggested by the frequency with which it has been performed since the 1950s and by the way that it has been applied to a wide number of similar situations in different cultures and periods. For example, Miller reported, in the *Detroit News*, a conversation he had with a Chinese woman writer who was imprisoned under the communist regime in her own country who said that "when she saw the play in 88 or 89 in Shanghai, she couldn't believe a non-Chinese had written it." The play speaks to anyone who has lived in a society where the questioning of authority and of the general opinion leads to rejection and punishment.

Author Biography

Arthur Miller was born on October 17, 1915, in New York City, the son of Isidore and Augusta Miller. His father lost his wealth during the Great Depression of the 1920s and the family, like many others, suffered economic hardship and could not afford to send him to college. Miller worked for two years in an automobile parts warehouse, earning enough money to attend the University of Michigan in 1934, where he studied history and economics. He graduated in 1938.

Benefitting from the U.S. Government's Federal Theatre Project, Miller began learning about the craft of the theatre, working with such skilled writers and directors as Clifford Odets (*Waiting for Lefty*) and Elia Kazan (the famous film and theatre director who later produced Miller's best-known work, *Death of a Salesman*). His first Broadway production, *The Man Who Had All the Luck*, opened in 1944 and ran for only four performances. After working as a journalist (work that included coverage of World War II) and writing a novel about anti-Semitism, Miller had his first real success on Broadway with *All My Sons* (1947); he followed this in 1949 with *Death of a Salesman*. Along with another early play, *A View from the Bridge*, and *The Crucible*, these are the plays for which Miller is best-known—though he has continued to write successfully, including a 1996 screenplay adaptation of *The Crucible* for a major motion picture.

In the 1940s and 1950s, because of his Jewish faith and his liberal political views, Miller was very much involved in contemporary debates that criticized the shortcomings of modern American society-particularly those dealing with inequalities in labor and race. It was also these political areas that were considered suspicious by Joseph McCarthy and his cronies, who sought to expose and erase Communism in America. Miller's association with people and organizations targeted by McCarthy's House Committee on Un-American Activities solidified his belief in the evils of blind persecution (while there may have been Communists who were bad people and a threat to America, this did not mean that all Communists were like-minded and posed a threat to the American way of life).

Earlier, Miller had written an adaptation of Henrik Ibsen's 1884 play, *An Enemy of the People*, which, according to his introduction, questioned "whether the democratic guarantees protecting political minorities ought to be set aside in time of crisis." As his later writing in *The Crucible* suggests, Miller did not believe that Communism was a threat that warranted the response provided by McCarthyism. U.S. authorities disagreed, however, and in 1954 when Miller was invited to Brussels to see a production of that play, the State Department denied him a visa. He then wrote a satirical piece called *A Modest Proposal for the Pacification of the Public Temper*, which denied that he supported the Communist cause. Nevertheless, he was called to appear before the House Un-American Activities Committee where, although his passport was conditionally restored, he nonetheless refused to give the names of people he had seen at Communist meetings. Because he refused to expose these people, Miller was found guilty of contempt of Congress in 1957.

In his personal life, Miller married Mary Grace Slattery in 1940; in 1956 they were divorced. In June 1956 he married Marilyn Monroe, the famous actress, and their marriage ended in 1961. Monroe subsequently committed suicide. Since 1962, Miller has been married to Ingeborg Morath, a photojournalist. He has four children, two each from his first and third marriages.

Plot Summary

Act 1

The play opens in Salem, Massachusetts, 1692, with the Reverend Samuel Parris praying over the bed of his daughter Betty. Abigail, his niece, enters with news from the Doctor that there is no explanation for Betty's inertia and disturbed state of mind. As their conversation progresses and he questions her, it is revealed that Betty has fallen into this state after her father found her in the woods dancing around a fire with Abigail, Tituba (Parris's slave from the island of Barbados), and other young women from the town. Parris warns Abigail that her reputation is already under suspicion as she has been dismissed from the service of Goody Proctor and has not been hired since. With the arrival of Goody Putnam, it is further revealed that her daughter Ruth is in a similar condition and that she was dancing in an attempt to communicate with her dead sisters.

Parris leaves to lead the recital of a psalm. Abigail reveals to Mercy, the Putnams' servant, that Mercy was seen naked. When Mary Warren, the Proctors' servant arrives, she suggests that they tell the truth and just be whipped for dancing, rather than risk being hanged for witchcraft. Betty wakes and tries to fly out of the window and then accuses Abigail of having drunk blood to make Goody

Proctor die. Abigail warns them not to say any more.

When the farmer John Proctor arrives, Abigail's flirtation with him (which he resists) suggests that she has been sexually involved with him in the past. She tells him that it is all pretense and that Betty is just scared. Meanwhile, a psalm can be heard from below and at the phrase "going up to Jesus," Betty cries out. Parris and the others rush into the room, interpreting Betty's outburst as a sign that witchcraft is at work in the young woman. Rebecca Nurse, a wise old woman, comforts Betty. Parris has sent for Reverend Hale, who has past experience with witchcraft; Hale arrives with his many books. Tituba is questioned, and after a considerable amount of pressure, names women who she has seen with the Devil. Joining in the hysterical atmosphere, which is beginning to prevail, Abigail adds more names to the list, as does Betty.

Act 2

The setting shifts to the home of the Proctors. Elizabeth Proctor tells John that Mary, their servant, keeps going to the court to take part in the trial proceedings which have begun in the eight days that have elapsed between Acts 1 and 2. Elizabeth begs John to reveal to the investigators what Abigail told him about it all being pretense, but he is unwilling. She is suspicious that this is because he has feelings for Abigail. The servant Mary returns from the court and gives Elizabeth a rag doll which she made while at the court. In the following angry conversation between Mary and John (who threatens to whip her), she reveals that Elizabeth has been accused but says that she spoke against the accusation.

Hale arrives and questions the Proctors. To prove that they are Christian people, he asks John to recite the Ten Commandments. Revealingly, given his recent liaison with Abigail, John can remember them all except "Thou shalt not commit adultery," which Elizabeth supplies for him. Giles Corey and Francis Nurse arrive and report that their wives have been taken to prison. Ezekiel Cheever, the clerk of the court, arrives and, seeing the doll, lifts up its skirt to reveal the needle which Mary left in the stomach after knitting. This he connects with Abigail's recent falling to the floor with stomach pains which were found to be caused by a needle. Mary notes that Abigail sat next to her in court while she made the puppet. When the others have gone, Proctor insists that Mary must tell the court what Abigail has been doing, but she refuses, saying that she is too scared. Proctor throws her onto the ground.

Act 3

In the courtroom, tensions and long-standing battles among members of the Salem community are brought to the fore, as Corey accuses Putnam of trying to take his land (which, were he convicted, he would be forced to sell and which Putnam would gladly purchase). Later in the scene Corey accuses Putnam of persuading his daughter to make accusations against George Jacobs so that his land would also be forfeited.

Proctor and Mary arrive and Mary confesses that the testimonies were a fabrication. Proctor is told that Elizabeth is pregnant and cannot be sentenced. Proctor presents a petition from members of the town supporting Elizabeth, Rebecca Nurse, and Martha Corey, but he is accused by Governor Danforth of undermining the court. Danforth then demands that all the people who have signed the petition be arrested.

Abigail, with her friends, denies lying and acts as if she is being bewitched by Mary. Proctor angrily pulls her by the hair and, to avoid her having any hold over him, confesses to adultery with her. Abigail denies this, and when Elizabeth is brought in, she does the same, thinking to protect her husband. Hale believes Proctor, but Danforth does not. To distract the proceedings when they seem to be turning against her, Abigail points upwards and claims to see a great bird in the rafters which she interprets as Mary trying to hurt her. The other girls join in the accusation and Mary gives in and takes their side, accusing Proctor of being on the side of the devil. He is arrested along with Giles Corey. Hale leaves after denouncing the entire proceedings.

Act 4

Parris informs the investigators that Abigail has taken money from his safe and left town. He fears rebellion among his congregation, only a few of whom came to the church to hear John Proctor's excommunication. Hale reasons that the accused must be pardoned since they have not confessed and describes how: "There are orphans wandering from house to house; abandoned cattle bellow on the highroads, the stink of rotting crops hands everywhere, and no man knows when the harlot's cry will end his life." However, Danforth refuses to give in as twelve people have already been hanged; he speaks of his determination to extract a confession from Proctor.

Proctor and Elizabeth are left to talk alone. She informs him that while many have confessed, Rebecca Nurse still refuses to do so. She also reveals that Giles Corey refused to answer the charge and died under the pressure of huge stones that were placed on his chest in an effort to torture him into confessing. His final words were "more weight." In the presence of the investigators who then return, Proctor is on the brink of confessing. When Rebecca is brought in to hear him and, the investigators hope, learn from his example, he changes his mind, refusing to name others and finally tearing up his confession. As the prisoners are taken away to be hanged, Parris rushes after them, and Hale pleads with Elizabeth to intervene. But she will not. The play ends with Hale weeping.

Characters

Ezekiel Cheever

Cheever is a tailor and a clerk of the court who places great importance in his job, which he sees as a holy one. He is at once fearful, embarrassed, apologetic, and a little officious. He discovers the doll that Mary knitted for Elizabeth Proctor. Discovering a needle in the doll's stomach, he believes that Elizabeth is practicing some kind of witchcraft that has affected Abigail.

Giles Corey

An old man, Giles Corey is "knotted with muscle, canny, inquisitive, and still powerful. . . . He didn't give a hoot for public opinion, and only in his last years did he bother much with the church. . . . He was a crank and a nuisance, but withal a deeply innocent and brave man." Corey refuses to answer the charges levied against him and is crushed to death beneath heavy stones that are placed upon his chest by the inquisitors, who are attempting to torture a confession out of him. Because he neither admitted the charge nor denied it and risked being hanged, his property passed to his sons instead of the town. His refusal to cooperate and his disdain for the trials is illustrated in his last words before he dies beneath the stones: "More weight."

Media Adaptations

- The first film version of *The Crucible* was made in France in 1957. It stars Simone Signoret, Yves Montand, Mylene Demongeot, and Jean Debucourt. The film was directed by Raymond Rouleau and written by Jean-Paul Sartre.

- No further film adaptations were made until 1996, when Miller's own screenplay of his drama was put into production by Twentieth Century Fox. Directed by Nicholas Hytner, the film stars Daniel Day-Lewis as Proctor, Winona Ryder as Abigail, and Joan Allen as Goody Proctor. In his introduction to the Penguin edition of the screenplay, Miller pointed to the advantages of film:"There was the possibility of showing the wild beauty of the newly cultivated land bordered by the wild sea, and the utter disorder and chaos of the town meetings where the people were busy condemning one another to death for loving the Evil One. Now one could show the hysteria as it grew rather than for the most part reporting it only."

- Several versions of a sound recording of *The Crucible* in the Lincoln Centre for the Performing Arts, New York, Repertory Theater are available and are published by Caedmon.

- *The Crucible* has also been made into an opera with music by Robert Ward and libretto by Bernard Stambler. Recordings of the New York City Opera performance have been produced by Composers Recordings and Troy Albany Records.

- In 1995 Penguin Books produced an interactive multimedia CD-ROM which includes a searchable text of the play, hypertext annotations, video interviews, historical data, pictorial material, commentary, and a bibliography.

Deputy Governor Danforth

Danforth is described as a "grave man of some humor and sophistication that does not, however, interfere with an exact loyalty to his position and his cause." Contrary to the strong and proficient appearance he puts forth, however, he is revealed to be, at times, distracted and uncomprehending of the proceedings over which he presides. Although, like Hale, he is presented with considerable evidence that Proctor and the others are innocent, he refuses to grant them clemency. He argues that it would reflect badly on the court if he released prisoners after executing a number of people accused of the same crimes—regardless of their innocence. He is a stubborn man who sees no flexibility in the law and whose pride and position will not allow him to reverse a previous decision.

Goody Sarah Good

Goody Good is a ragged and crazy woman who seems to live on the edges of town life. Although past child-bearing age, she is thought to be pregnant. The fact that she is eventually jailed as a witch suggests how eager the townspeople are to condemn anyone who does not conform to the accepted norms of their community.

Reverend John Hale

Hale embodies many of the moral

contradictions of the play: he is a man of integrity who, although at times misguided and overzealous, is willing to change his mind when confronted with the truth. Despite this admirable trait, he lacks the moral conviction to act against proceedings that will condemn innocents to death. He comes to realize that John Proctor is guilty of nothing more than adultery yet he lacks the courage to question the decisions of the court and the prevailing attitude of seventeenth century society. While his fair-mindedness and humanity deserve a measure of respect, Hale's inability to perceive—and endorse— the power in Proctor's stand for personal virtue leaves his character ignorant and weak.

Judge Hathorne

Hathorne is a "bitter, remorseless Salem judge" who has bigotted views although he appears courteous and respectful on the surface.

Marshall Herrick

Herrick seems to be the gentle and courteous side of law enforcement in Salem. He follows the law carefully, treats people gently, and has the respect of the townspeople. Despite this, he is still a participant in the inquisition that results in the executions of numerous residents.

Mercy Lewis

The Putnam's servant, Mercy Lewis is

described as "a fat, sly, merciless girl." She quickly follows Abigail in her accusations and finds a power and confidence in accusation which contrasts with her usually fearful demeanor.

Francis Nurse

Nurse is a hard-working, honest member of the community who is shocked by his wife, Rebecca's arrest. Both he and his wife are shown to be kindly town elders who, before the accusations fly, are highly respected and liked by all. He is more or less an innocent bystander whose life is turned upside down by the hysteria that grips Salem.

Goody Rebecca Nurse

When Rebecca is accused of witchcraft it becomes clear that the town has lapsed into collective madness as she stands out uniquely as a woman of great wisdom, compassion, and moral strength. She is gentle and loving, deeply spiritual, and a mother of eleven children and twenty-six grandchildren. Her moral character and strong sense of her own goodness is evident in her adamant refusal to sign a confession. When she is brought into the room where John Proctor is about to sign his confession, her presence proves pivotal in Proctor's decision to take a stand for integrity and not sign the confession.

Betty Parris

Reverend Parris's daughter, Betty, is caught up in the fear and accusations which are generated after the girls are discovered dancing in the woods. It is not revealed whether her illness is feigned or if it is a genuine physical response to a traumatic situation, but it is clear that she is easily influenced and deeply affected by her experiences.

Reverend Samuel Parris

Parris, Salem's minister, and Abigail's uncle, is a weak character who appears to enjoy and to be protective of the status which his position brings. This aspect of his personality is evident in his dispute about whether the provision of his firewood should be take out of his salary or is extra to it. He is concerned with appearances, and, when interrogating Abigail about her dealings with witches in the opening scene, he seems to worry more about what these activities will mean to his reputation than Abigail's spiritual state. He continues to follow public opinion right to the end of the play, when he insists that Proctor's confession must be made publicly in order for it to be effective.

Goody Elizabeth Proctor

Although both her husband and Abigail remark on her coolness, Elizabeth is gentle and devoted to her family. Her goodness and dignity are evident in the way that she argues calmly against Hale and Danforth's accusations. Her loyalty to John is most clearly demonstrated when, thinking to protect him, she denies that he has committed adultery. Her acceptance of John's decision to recant his confession further illustrates her wisdom and her ability to grasp the wider issues of morality and personal integrity for which her husband is willing to die.

John Proctor

The central figure in the play, Proctor is an ordinary man, a blunt farmer who speaks his mind and is often ruled by his passions. It is revealed early in the play that he has had an adulterous affair with Abigail, who worked as his servant. Yet he clearly shows remorse for his act and is attempting to right his error; he is conciliatory with his wife, Elizabeth, and disdainful of Abigail's sexual advances.

When the accusations fly at the trials, he is determined to tell the truth, even if it means criticizing and antagonizing the investigators. His determination to expose Abigail's false accusations eventually leads him to admit his own adultery to the court. He is at his most self-aware in his final speech when he realizes the importance of maintaining his integrity. Explaining why he has recanted his confession, he cries: "Because it is my name! Because I cannot have another in my life! Because I lie and sign myself to lies! Because I am not worth the dust on the feet of them that hang! How may I live without my name? I have given you my soul, leave me my name!"

Goody Ann Putnam

Goody Putnam is "a twisted soul. . . a death-ridden woman haunted by bad dreams." The death of all of her children has affected her deeply. Her pain has been turned into a vindictiveness which is directed at Rebecca Nurse.

Thomas Putnam

Putnam is "a well-to-do hard-handed landowner" who attempts to benefit from the accusations made against other members of the community. Giles Corey accuses him of taking advantage of accused landowners' plights. Knowing that the convicted will be forced to sell their land for much less than it is worth, Putnam is all too eager to attain these properties at cut-rate prices. He has many grievances, and his vengeful, angry behavior seems to stem from his desire for power and possessions.

Tituba

Tituba is Reverend Parris's black slave and a native of the island of Barbados. She is suspected of black magic due to the traditions of Voodoo that were prevalent in her home country. She is genuinely fond of Abigail and Betty. The events bring out her superstitious nature, and her fears become uncontrolled, eventually degenerating into madness when she is in jail.

Susanna Walcott

Susanna Walcott is carried along by the hysteria of the other girls, enjoying the attention which they get from making accusations. Otherwise she is nervous and tense.

Mary Warren

Mary Warren is the Proctors' servant who seems timid and subservient but who finds a powerful role in a kind of people's jury in the courtroom. She occasionally dares to defy Proctor, particularly in her insistence that she must attend the hearings, but she is easily intimidated into at least partial submission. Proctor convinces her that she must expose Abigail's lies to the court, which she agrees to do. She becomes hysterical before the court, however, and soon joins Abigail in pretending that there is evil witchcraft at work. Her behavior in the court contributes, in part, to John Proctor's arrest.

Abigail Williams

In the character of Abigail are embodied many of the main issues of the play. Her accusations initially reveal a mischievous enjoyment in wielding power over other people's lives. But the fact that the events which they set in motion seem to far outweigh the initial mischief suggests that the community of Salem has embedded in its fabric elements of social corruption, moral disease, or unresolved and repressed feelings of anger and hostility. Abigail's actions should be seen as an effect rather than a cause of the town's accusatory environment.

It is noteworthy that, because her parents were brutally killed, she is without adults to whom she is close: Parris cares for her material needs, but there is no evidence that they are emotionally close or that he provides her with anything but the most basic of guidance. Her adulterous relationship with John Proctor might be seen as a craving for affection which, in the absence of family love, manifests itself in physical desire. Her eventual escape to Boston where it is reported she became a prostitute suggests the same craving for emotional love through physical intimacy. Abigail's apparent belief in witchcraft may have similar roots to her sexual neediness. It is psychologically plausible that she would need to find an alternative to the strict and, it seems, loveless Puritanism of her uncle, and that this would attract her to precisely the things— black magic, physical expression, and sexual conjuring—which the religion of her community forbids (she craved attention regardless of whether it was positive or negative attention). She is at once a frightening and pitiable character, malicious in her accusations and sad in her need for close human contact and attention.

Themes

Politics

In the early 1950s, hearings at Senator Joseph McCarthy's powerful House Un-American Activities Committee had decided that the American Communist Party, a legal political party, was compromising the security of the nation by encouraging connections with Russia (America's ally during the Second World War but its enemy afterwards). Those who were sympathetic to the communist cause, or those who had connections with Russia, were summoned before the committee to explain their involvement, recant their beliefs, and name their former friends and associates in the communist cause. Miller himself had to attend a Senate hearing in 1957. He admitted that he had been to communist meetings—of writers—but refused to name anyone else. He denied having been a member of the Party and was eventually found guilty of contempt.

Topics for Further Study

- What is your perception of the girls' allegations in the play? Do they really believe in witchcraft or are they fabricating the events?

- Is John Proctor a tragic figure? Compare his fate to that of such tragic literary figures as King Oedipus in Sophocles's *Oedipus Rex* and the title character in William Shakespeare's *Hamlet*.

- Examine the historical facts regarding the Salem Witch Trials and Joseph McCarthy's hearings. In what ways does Miller employ these facts in the service of his drama. How do the two historical events compare to each other?

- What purpose do Miller's authorial

prose inserts in the text serve?

- Miller said that "McCarthyism may have been the historical occasion of the play, not its theme." What other political and social events do you perceive the play addressing?

The McCarthy Committee's antagonism of innocent (and in most cases harmless) citizens—and politically-motivated persecution in general—is explored in *The Crucible* through the subject of witchcraft. Particularly, through the dramatization of events which took place in Salem, Massachusetts, in the seventeenth century. The town's hysteria at the beginning of the play has a direct parallel in the frenzy that communist "witch-hunting" caused in America in the 1950s. Further, John Proctor's trial, confession (obtained through antagonism and threats), and ultimate recantation conjures a scene similar to the ones that were played out in front of the House Un-American Activities Committee. By having his protagonist take a stand for his beliefs and his personal integrity, Miller displays a clear sympathy for those persecuted in McCarthy's inquisition. The playwright's message is one of personal and political freedom for every citizen.

The Crucible also examines political persecution as a tool for deflecting attention away from difficult problem areas. McCarthy's persecution of communist sympathizers did little to strengthen the fiber of American life (quite conversely, it added unwelcome suspicion and paranoia to many people's lives). To many, however, his actions made McCarthy look like an avenging hero for capitalism and diverted the American public's attention away from very real problems such as race and gender inequities. The investigators in Miller's play act in a very similar manner: They refuse to face the idea that their strict way of life may have led several young women to rebel (by, for example, dancing around a fire in the woods). Instead they blame the wayward girls' actions on the Devil and witchcraft. With this action they bond the community together in a battle against an outside evil that has corrupted their town. Unfortunately, in much the same way that McCarthy's persecution ultimately unraveled many American communities, the Salem Witch Trials end up destroying a way of life in the village.

Morals and Morality

The issues which *The Crucible* raises have general moral relevance, as well as being related directly to the situation in America at the time the play was written. As Dennis Welland has noted in his *Arthur Miller*, the play's moral is similar to those often found in the works of George Bernard Shaw (*Pygmalion, Major Barbara*). Shaw's morals often contend that wrong-headed actions—such as the witch trials—are often motivated by a lack of personal responsibility rather than based upon deliberate cruelty or malice. That is, rather than take a stand against proceedings they suspect are unjust, the townspeople of Salem go along with the trials. Welland stated: "That is why Elizabeth quietly rejects as 'the Devil's argument' Hale's impassioned plea to her to help Proctor save himself . . . Elizabeth, like [George Bernard] Shaw's St Joan [in his play of that name], has learnt through suffering that 'God's most precious gift is not life at any price, but the life of spiritual freedom and moral integrity.' In Proctor's final recantation of his confession and his refusal to put his principles aside to save his life, we see the triumph of personal integrity in a world of moral uncertainty."

Society

Paralleling Miller's exploration of individual morality is his portrayal of society's response to events within its community. In the girls' initial accusations and the frenzy that ensues, Miller demonstrates how peer pressure can lead individuals into taking part in actions which they know are wrong. And in the community's reaction to these accusations, he shows how easily stories can be taken out of context—and how people are blamed for crimes they haven't committed. Miller links the mass hysteria of Salem to the community's excessive religious zeal and very strict attitudes towards sex. Sexual relationships and other instances of physical expression seem on the surface to be repressed and the fact that the girls fear being whipped for dancing and singing suggests the strict codes of behavior under which they live.

Yet the town is not without its sexual scandal: Abigail and John Proctor's adulterous relationship is very much in the foreground of the play and is a factor in the unfolding of the tragic events. It may be that Miller is suggesting that such strict religious codes lead to the repression of feelings which eventually escape and find expression in forbidden forms of behavior. The mass hysteria of the young girls could be seen as an outbreak of sexual feelings and fantasies which have long been repressed.

Nicholas Hytner (*The Madness of King George*), the director of the 1996 film adaptation of *The Crucible* (for which Miller wrote the screenplay) pointed out this element when he noted in his introduction to the Penguin edition of the screenplay that "a community that denies to its young any outlet for the expression of sexuality is asking for trouble." Through the events of the play, Miller seems to be warning against excessive religious (as well as political) fanaticism by showing the potential outbursts of feelings—and the disastrous results—which can occur if all forms of sexual expression are repressed.

The Meaning in Miller's Title

The title *The Crucible* hints at paradoxical concerns which run throughout the play. On the one hand, a crucible, as a melting pot in which metals are heated to separate out the base metals from the valuable ones, could represent the spiritual improvement which can happen to human beings as a result of trials and hardship. On the other hand, a crucible is also a witches' cauldron in which ingredients are brewed together to be used in black magic. In this sense, Miller might be suggesting that good can even come out of attempted evil, as well as the normal and healthy challenges of Christian life. In this sense, the events in Salem are seen as a necessary evil which roots out evil at the very heart of the community and which brings about a kind of cleansing; the events in Salem had to occur so that they would not be repeated in subsequent times.

Prose Inserts

To understand how *The Crucible* might be performed, and to appreciate it as a text as well as a script, it is helpful to examine Miller's prose inserts, which explain the action which is taking place in the dialogue. In his directions, Miller leaves very little room for interpretation; in almost didactic terms, he spells out the background to the witch trials and fleshes out characters, focusing particularly on their motives and the psychological states that lead them to be swept along by the tragedy. For example, early in Act 1 Miller provides a quick thumbnail sketch of Thomas Putnam which explains his grievances about land and the way the town is run and gives details of his vindictive and embittered nature. This information helps the reader to appreciate Putnam's desire to gain land and status later on in the play; by giving this background information, Miller encourages the reader to feel little sympathy for the greedy old man when he and his wife carry on with the accusations which their daughter (herself an obviously disturbed child) helps to set in motion. For a viewer watching the play, these facets of Putnam's character must be conveyed by the actor, but for the reader or the actor, they provide a useful framework.

Language

Historical realism is suggested by the language which Miller employs for his characters' speech. It is the language of the seventeenth century East Coast settlers and is often highly conversational. The women's language is particularly rich in jargon: for example, Rebecca Nurse says that she will "go to God for you" which means that she will pray, and Mrs. Putnam says "mark it for a sign" which means that she thinks that something is a sign from God. By using this language, which is significantly out of time from contemporary standards, Miller establishes the historical distance of the events. This helps the reader or viewer to imagine the strict nature of society and the manner in which religion permeated nearly every facet of the villagers' lives.

Reported Speech

Because neither the events in the woods nor in the courtroom are actually seen in the play, this information is provided by characters' reports of what has happened. The viewer or reader must piece together an understanding of the events and of the vested interest of those reporting. This is particularly apparent in the very first scene where the audience must figure out why Betty is lying in bed in a catatonic state, why Tituba is trying to reassure herself and others that everything will be alright, and why Reverend Parris is so angry. When reading the text, it is helpful to ask not only who is speaking and to whom, but also what motives they have for describing things the way they do to this particular person and at this time.

Miller warns in the preface to *The Crucible* that "this play is not history," but it is certainly dependent on historical events for its story. It will be necessary in this section to deal with two periods of history: first the time of the Salem witch trials and second the time of McCarthyism in the 1950s when Miller was writing.

Marion Starkey's 1949 book, *The Witch Trials in Massachusetts* first generated interest in the events that took place in Salem, Massachusetts, in the seventeenth century. Those accused of witchcraft were hounded by representatives of their community (and the larger pressure of majority opinion) until they admitted their involvement, naming others involved in suspicious practices— although the majority of those accused and named were guilty of nothing more than behavior that did not conform to the societal norms of the time.

Despite what might be obvious to contemporary readers as free expression or eccentricity, these people were nevertheless prosecuted in Salem. Spearheaded by the crusade of the real-life Reverend Parris, twenty people were killed based on the suspicion that they had involvement with witchcraft. A good number of these people were killed for refusing to cooperate with the proceedings, having never confessed to any crimes. The Salem Witch Trials stand as an example of religious hysteria and mob mentality in American history.

Miller carefully uses this historical information as the basis for his play. The language of contemporary seventeenth century religious practice, which he frequently employs, demonstrates the thoroughness of his historical research into the customs of this period. For example, Parris points out at one point that "we are not Quakers." The Puritans disapproved of the Quakers because they believed that God could speak to individuals and inspire them to communicate on his behalf. Consequently, the Quakers avoided hierarchical forms of church government. The Puritans, in contrast, believed that God would only speak through his ordained ministers and accordingly placed great importance on their work. Further references include Abigail's comment about "these Christian women and their covenanted men" which reminds the audience that Puritans had to swear a solemn promise to accept the rules of the Church before they could become full members; and Proctor's criticism of Parris's fondness for highly decorated churches—"This man dreams cathedrals, not clapboard meetin' houses"; Puritans were not supposed to value this kind of decoration which was traditionally associated with other Christian denominations, particularly Roman Catholicism. *The Crucible* is steeped in the language and customs of seventeenth century east coast America.

Compare & Contrast

- **1600s:** Puritan settlers in New England, familiar with persecution, create tightly-knit communities where church and state are closely linked in the running of the society. In *The Crucible* Miller described the state which they created as "a theocracy, a combine of state and religious power whose function was to keep the community together and to prevent any kind of disunity that might open it up to destruction by material or ideological enemies."

1953: Joseph Stalin, ruler of the Soviet Union since 1928, dies at the age of 73. Hostilities with the West continue and in the U.S. attempts are made through the House Committee on Un-American Activities to root out communists in America.

Today: The end of the Cold War has seen the breakdown of a communist influence in Eastern Europe as well as the fragmentation of the Soviet Union into smaller independent states. Barriers between Russia and the U.S. have also largely disappeared and, although not allies, the two countries negotiate on matters such as world peace and world trade.

- **1600s:** Puritans in the seventeenth century believe in three different kinds of witchcraft: "white magic" which involves the use of charms and spells to bring good luck; "black magic" which utilizes spells and incantations to harm others; and Satanic servitude, which involves dedicating one's life in the service of the Devil. Whether or not witchcraft really exists, the effects of these beliefs on the community are great, and considerable fear is generated.

1953: The Church of Scientology is founded in Washington D.C. by science fiction writer L. Ron Hubbard, who bases his philosophy on the belief that man is a free spirit who can achieve his true nature only by freeing himself from the emotional trappings of the past. Accusations that Scientology is not a true religion and that the organization uses intimidation tactics to extract money from its followers are widespread. Other controversial religious sects, including the Reverend Sun Myung Moon's Unification Church (commonly referred to as the

Moonies), also form in the following decades.

Today: Numerous cults and religious subsets exist all over the world. They are generally tolerated in free and liberal societies, but recent events involving mass suicides of such cults as the Branch Davidians in Waco, Texas, the Heaven's Gate group in California, and the nerve gas bombing by the Aum Shinrikyo ("Supreme Truth") in Japan, have raised concerns about the influence of such cults, particularly on people who are young, impressionable, or socially isolated.

Running parallel to these early events are those that took place in Miller's own time, on which the playwright symbolically comments through the story of the witch trials. Miller was interested in political issues, including communism, which had developed after the Second World War when Russia's communist government became a significant world power. In the early 1950s, hearings at Senator Joseph McCarthy's House Un-American Activities Committee had decided that the American Communist Party, a legal political party, was compromising the security of the nation by encouraging connections with Russia. Those who were sympathetic to the communist cause, or those who had connections with Russia, could be summoned before the committee to explain their involvement, recant their beliefs, and name their former friends and associates in the communist cause.

Of particular interest to the committee were those practicing communists in the artistic community. Reasoning that the most nefarious methods for converting Americans to communist beliefs would be through the films, music, and art that they enjoyed, McCarthy and his cohorts prosecuted a great many playwrights, screenwriters, and other artists. In a number of cases they were successful in "blacklisting" these artists—which meant that no one would purchase their services for fear of being linked to communism. This event had its highest profile in the Hollywood of the 1950s, when such screenwriters as Dalton Trumbo (*Spartacus*) and Ben Hecht (*Notorious*) were denied employment by major studios (although a great number of blacklisted talents continued to write using "fronts"—legitimate writers who would put their name on the blacklisted author's work). A number of Miller's contemporaries lost their livelihood due to these hearings, and the playwright himself was brought before the proceedings.

These themes are explored in *The Crucible* through the subject of witchcraft and social hysteria. In the town's hysteria at the beginning of the play lies a parallel to the frenzy that communist "witch-hunting" caused in America in the 1950s. And in

John Proctor's trial, confession, recantation, and refusal to name his associates, are incidents which regularly occurred in front of the House Un-American Activities Committee. However, because of its broad sweep of moral themes, the play has also had a life beyond the immediate and specific historical circumstances for which it was written. For example, its themes have been applied to such diverse subjects as religious fanaticism in the late-twentieth century, child abuse accusations in the U.S. and in Europe, and political freedom in Eastern Europe and China. While McCarthyism had been Miller's inspiration, the play's themes address many different circumstances in which mob mentality overrides personal integrity and placing blame on scapegoats proves easier than confronting (and correcting) deep-rooted societal inadequacies. As long as such practices ensue, the play's historical context will continue to be revised and reapplied.

Critical Overview

In its initial production in 1953, *The Crucible* received a mixed reception from drama critics, with many complaining that, while sturdy in its craftsmanship, the work was too obviously a morality play and lacked the adventurousness and innovation of his previous work. Critic Richard Hayes wrote in the *Commonweal: "The Crucible*, does not, I confess, seem to me a work of such potential tragic force as the playwright's earlier *Death of a Salesman;* it is the product of theatrical dexterity and a young man's moral passion, rather than of a fruitful and reverberating imagination. But it has, in a theatre of the small success and the tidy achievement, power, the passionate line—an urgent boldness which does not shrink from the implications of a large and formidable design." George Jean Nathan saw similar aspects of Miller's work, writing in his 1953 *Theatre Arts* review: *"The Crucible*, in sum, is an honorable sermon on a vital theme that misses because the sting implicit in it has been disinfected with an editorial tincture and because, though it contains the potential deep vibrations of life, it reduces them to mere superficial tremors."

In addition to being compared to *Death of a Salesman, The Crucible's* debut also suffered due to the play's thinly veiled criticism of McCarthyism; many were too embarrassed or afraid to speak publicly or attend performances of the work.

Nonetheless, it received numerous honors, including the Antoinette ("Tony") Perry Award and the Donaldson Award in 1953 as well as the Obie Award from the *Village Voice* in 1958.

The play reopened after the McCarthy era and has continued to be successful since then. In 1964 critic Herbert Blau noted that a competent production of the play virtually guaranteed good box office sales, and indeed it has been in almost continuous performance since the early 1960s. *The Crucible* is a particularly popular school text in both the U.S. and Britain. In *Modern Drama*, critic Robert A. Martin summed up the popularity of Miller's play when he noted that it "has endured beyond the immediate events of its own time. . . . As one of the most frequently produced plays in the American theater, *The Crucible* has attained a life of its own; one that both interprets and defines the cultural and historical background of American society. Given the general lack of plays in the American theater that have seriously undertaken to explore the meaning and significance of the American past in relation to the present, *The Crucible* stands virtually alone as a dramatically coherent rendition of one of the most terrifying chapters in American history."

Critic Henry Popkin also discussed the perpetual appeal of *The Crucible* in an essay in *College English*. While the critic did not see the depth of universality in human and political themes that Martin wrote of, Popkin did express admiration for Miller's skill in creating human characters with whom audiences continue to identify. Explaining the play's appeal as a well-crafted drama, the critic wrote: *"The Crucible* keeps our attention by furnishing exciting crises, each one proceeding logically from its predecessor, in the lives of people in whom we have been made to take an interest. That is a worthy intention, if it is a modest one, and it is suitably fulfilled."

The 1996 film version of *The Crucible* won generally favorable reviews for its attention to detail. The adaptation was also lauded for the skill with which events such as the courtroom scenes, which are not depicted (only verbally reported) in the play, were successfully turned into large-scale crowd scenes which fully utilized the possibilities of film. Commenting on the durability of Miller's tale, Richard Corliss wrote in *Time* that *"The Crucible* offers solid workmanship and familiar epiphanies." Yet the critic also noted that Hytner and his actors have provided new perceptions of the characters for a contemporary audience. Discussing the erotic energy of Winona Ryder's portrayal of Abigail, Corliss stated that "Ryder exposes the real roots of the piece. Forget McCarthyism; *The Crucible* is a colonial *Fatal Attraction."* Reviewing the film for *Newsweek*, David Ansen saw the film's effectiveness emanating from the work's original themes, writing, "Miller has revised his venerable opus, quickening its rhythms for the screen, but what works is what's always worked when this play is well produced: you feel pity, horror, moral outrage."

Sources

Ansen, David. "One Devil of a Time" in *Newsweek*, December 2, 1996, p. 80.

Corliss, Richard. "Going All the Way" in *Time*, Vol. 148, no. 25, December 2, 1996, p. 81.

Hayes, Richard. Review of *The Crucible* in the *Commonweal*, Vol. LVII, no. 20, February 20, 1953, p. 498.

Interview with Arthur Miller in the *Detroit News*, October 26, 1996, p. 1C.

Martin, Robert A. "Arthur Miller's *The Crucible:* Background and Sources" in *Modern Drama*, September, 1977, pp. 279-92.

Nathan, George Jean. "Henrik Miller" in *Theatre Arts*, Vol. XXXVII, no. 4, April, 1953, pp. 24-26.

Popkin, Henry. "Arthur Miller's *The Crucible*" in *College English*, Vol. 26, no. 2, November, 1964, pp. 139-46.

Welland, Dennis. *Arthur Miller*, Oliver & Boyd, 1961.

Further Reading

Budick, E. Miller. "History and Other Specters in *The Crucible*" in *Arthur Miller*, edited by Harold Bloom, Chelsea House (New York), 1987.

> Budick discusses the role of John Proctor and the questions of personal morality and integrity.

Herron, Ima Honaker. *The Small Town in American Drama*, Southern Methodist University Press (Dallas), 1969.

> Herron discusses different portrayals of American small town life, focusing on *The Crucible* in her chapter on "The Puritan Village and the Common Madness of the Time."

Miller, Arthur. Introduction to his *The Crucible: Screenplay*, Viking Penguin, 1996.

> In his introduction, Miller provides some insights into the production of the 1996 film adaptation of his legendary play. He also discusses the text as a work that would appeal to modern audiences, citing a number of contemporary issues that the play addresses.

Starkey, Marion L. *The Witch Trials in Massachusetts*, Knopf (New York), 1949.

This book came out before Miller's play and was one of the first works to generate interest in the Salem Witch Trials. Starkey works with documents about the trial, which were collected together in the 1930s, and draws parallels with the 1940s, including the atrocities in Nazi Germany.

Warshow, Robert. "The Liberal Conscience in *The Crucible*" in *Essays in the Modern Drama*, edited by Freedman and Morris.

Warshow discusses the character of Hale and questions of social control and individual freedom.

CPSIA information can be obtained
at www.ICGtesting.com
Printed in the USA
LVOW13s1746311017
554455LV00010B/622/P